My Name is DeShawn: Assessing the Need for Affirmative Action

- Is there a need for the existence of this policy?
- To what extent is Affirmative Action effective?
- How is Affirmative Action a useful tool in reducing crime?
- What is the correlation between an individual's name and socio-economic status?
- Is there a need for race-based Affirmative Action resulting from discrimination?

Parbej Ali

Contents

Abstract

This text assesses the need for Affirmative Action policy for ethnic minorities within the United States. It attempts to clarify if there is a need for the existence of Affirmative Action policy by examining the reasons for its creation and whether these factors are relevant today. This text will attempt to establish to what extent affirmative action is needed to reduce social and economic inequalities in society by examining the effects of the policy on ethnic minorities. It will discuss the effectiveness and implementation of the policy and whether it achieves it intended outcomes. It will also research the impact of the policy and what implications its creation has had on employment attitudes and culture amongst the group it was created to help. By establishing a rationale for its continued existence, it shall be demonstrated that a complete lack of the policy is detrimental to equitable outcomes in society. Furthermore, by showing that there are unconsidered variables which traditional studies have until now neglected, a new model for resolving the situation of socio-economic disparity may be achieved. This is produced by examining the correlation between possessing a distinctive name that implies an ethnic origin together with a low social and economic class that results in a signalling mechanism that allows employers to screen out applicants. This warrants investigation as to whether this behaviour is the result of systemic discrimination against either race or class arising from perceptions about such names and is examined by looking at audit surveys of employers and admissions tutors for universities. The text concludes that due to societal asymmetries that still exist between demographic groups there is a need for Affirmative Action policy. However, its method of implementation may require modification and the removal of the policy is not a desirable option as it does not lead to equitable outcomes. This text cannot show definitively that discrimination still exists in the American system and is the cause of failures in Affirmative Action policy.

Title - My Name is DeShawn: Assessing the Need for Affirmative Action

Research Questions - In order to structure the text and provide an assessment of Affirmative Action, the following issues must be investigated:

<u>Is there a need for the existence of this policy?</u>

The policy currently exists and it is necessary to understand why it was created before it can be assessed if it is still needed for the same reasons.

<u>To what extent is Affirmative Action effective?</u>

It is necessary to assess what Affirmative Action achieves and whether or not its results are efficacious, or if the policy requires modification.

<u>How is Affirmative Action a useful tool in reducing crime?</u>

It is possible that Affirmative Action may have secondary consequences that are not naturally considered by policymakers and advocates.

<u>What is the correlation between an individual's name and socio-economic status?</u>

This question attempts to understand the results of various audit studies on the subject.

<u>Is there a need for race-based Affirmative Action resulting from discrimination?</u>

The aim of this question is to ascertain whether Affirmative Action requires race based initiatives in order to improve its effectiveness.

Methodology

Typically studies of Affirmative Action attempt to assess the impact the policy has on society by looking at its effectiveness and exploring whether it can reduce economic disparities in terms of employment and income, or lead to more minority groups gaining higher standards of education that they would otherwise have been able to receive. These assessments attempt to establish that quality standards are unaffected while greater quantities of minority groups are integrated into the system. This research aims to show that while these are positive benefits for society, Affirmative Action makes little impact in reducing the socio-economic problems and that the problems which lead to the original creation of the race-based sections of the policy have not been adequately addressed. Therefore, a solution to an existing problem has been created but is based upon incorrect assumptions and thus will never truly be able to correct any societal asymmetries that exist. It will assess the impact merit and aspiration may have on a person's outcomes and goals and how a lack of these may lead toward criminal activity. This work acknowledges that Affirmative Action usually applies to a wider field, including women's rights; however, the scope will be limited to investigating ethnic minorities in the United States of America with particular focus on the African-American population and whether there is a requirement for race-based initiatives within the Affirmative Action framework due to African-Americans being at a possible greater disadvantage than White Americans. This work focuses largely on the Californian experience of Affirmative Action, in part due to the *Californian*

Civil Rights Initiative that has led to much academic debate and other constitutional rulings that have had nationwide implications. As a result, the work is not a comparative piece but rather an assessment of how the policy has attempted to achieve its goals, given how it can function within the American legislative framework. It will not assess the effectiveness of Affirmative Action in aiding minorities into housing in neighbourhoods. For the purposes of this work, quantitative data is derived from many secondary sources such as audit studies as the scope of the project would not allow this type of work to conduct primary surveys due to insufficient time and funding. Many of these studies are socio-economic and correlative analyses on the subject of Affirmative Action. However, in order to explain much of the correlative evidence that will be investigated, the causal factors behind them are best explained through the use of qualitative information that is derived from political analysis. An outline of the historical context of the oppression of African-Americans and the history of Affirmative Action and subsequent rulings on the issue of race relations in America will be provided through discourse analysis. It is necessary that the work is organised in this manner from an epistemological point so that the present data takes into account how it is possible the situation came to be as it currently is and what appropriate policy suggestions and implications this should have for the future of Affirmative Action policies.

Background Context

Affirmative Action is a policy decision made by political institutions which aims to reduce disparity in socio-economic status by promoting access to education and employment (and in some cases, housing) for non-dominant groups in society such as women and ethnic minorities. The policy attempts to reduce discrimination that may exist within the system and provide restitution to affected minority groups. It exists as a result of these groups typically having lower income and education levels due to barriers of entry to employment and education (SEP: 2005). Affirmative Action acts as a tool to correct what is perceived to be an existing societal problem for these groups. It does not necessarily address how or why these groups are in what is perceived to be a less desirable socio-economic position than the dominant group or what may perpetuate this situation. Some Affirmative Action directives are used to promote diversity in an institution and this can usually be seen in university admissions and some workplaces. Access may be promoted via such methods as quotas or incentives for firms and institutions. When this has been judicially mandated it has been considered "hard" Affirmative Action, as opposed to "soft" Affirmative Action that is voluntarily undertaken by institutions. This has lead to some claims of reverse-discrimination against perhaps more deserving members of society from the dominant social groups who may also be innocent of any discrimination against members of a minority group perceived to be disproportionately benefiting from the policy (Anderson 2004: 77).

Decisions such as *Hopwood v Texas* (1992) have done much to scrutinize and curtail the effects of Affirmative Action policy as it once existed during the initial stages of its development (Anderson 2004: 253). Affirmative Action has now become a hugely contentious issue in America, particularly in regards to whether there is a need for race-based Affirmative Action policy. This has accelerated as a result of the "The Californian Civil Rights Initiative", better known as Proposition 209 that was proposed in 1996 by an African-American, Ward Connerly, claiming that Affirmative Action policy that took race into consideration assumed inferiority and inadequacy on the part of all African-Americans, instead arguing that Affirmative Action should solely be based on socio-economic factors so that the stigma attached to this issue was reduced (Connerly 2006). This, however, has resulted in many other states challenging the federally mandated policy. As a result, it is necessary to establish if there may be a need for such a policy by determining whether race is a limiting factor for the advancement of ethnic minority groups and whether Affirmative Action is an appropriate tool to help them out of this situation.

Structure

Chapter One addresses the first research question by examining the historical oppression particularly against African-Americans providing a justification for the need and creation of Affirmative Action.

Chapter Two examines why Affirmative Action is still needed in the education system and examines socio-economic asymmetries that still exist in order to provide an argument for the continued need for this policy. It also shows how it may help in reducing unwanted negative externalities in society, such as reducing crime.

Chapter Three attempts to explain the findings of various audit studies that suggest a person's name can work against them in the job market and thus may highlight a continuing discrimination problem. As a result, it will show that Affirmative Action does not target the cause of the problems in the American systems and that a name such as DeShawn is reflective of one's background.

Chapter Four suggests that removing Affirmative Action has an adverse effect on ethnic minority aspirations due to their perceptions of society and has in effect become institutionalised within the system.

Chapter Five provides an assessment of Affirmative Action as it stands in America and addresses its effectiveness as a policy.

01 A History of Oppression

"You do not wipe away the scars of centuries by saying: 'now, you are free to go where you want, do as you desire, and choose the leaders you please.' You do not take a man who for years has been hobbled by chains, liberate him, bring him to the starting line of a race, saying, 'you are free to compete with all the others,' and still justly believe you have been completely fair. This is the next and more profound stage of the battle for Civil Rights. We seek not just freedom but opportunity—not just legal equity but human ability—not just equality as a right and a theory, but equality as a fact and as a result."

President Johnson's Speech at Harvard University defining the concept of Affirmative Action (04 June 1965)

In 1790, the Congress of the United States passed the Naturalization Act which extended citizenship solely to free white men. Although small modifications were made to the legislation, the full extent of the racial qualification aspect of the Act remained until 1952 (Delgado: 2001: 76), though African-Americans had received the removal of limiting barriers in 1870 to some extent when Amendment XV was added to the constitution, stating that a person who had previously been a slave should be allowed to vote. This built on Amendment XIV which reversed the Supreme Court's Dred Scott ruling over Sanford of 1856 by Congress. As a result, Amendment XV rectified the issue that African-

Americans could not be citizens of the United States. Often this meant members of the Judiciary ruling that slaves (whom were typically of African origin) as well as people originating from Asia and the Persian Gulf could not qualify as "white men" and thus were not to receive the same treatment as many Europeans who found it easy to immigrate to the United States with few problems (Delgado 2001: 77). As result, it became clear from the early stages of the creation of the United States that there would be systemic discrimination and disadvantages placed on non-whites.

Historically in America the oppression of non-whites politically and economically has meant that in terms of social capital this has led to African-Americans and other non-whites being at a disadvantage in the contemporary arena

(Jones 2005: 43-55). African-Americans were heavily discriminated against well into the mid-twentieth century. After years of abuse, this culminated in a flashpoint incident on December 1, 1955 when African-American seamstress and member of the Nation Association for the Advancement of Colored People (NAACP) Rosa Parks refused to give up her seat on a segregated bus in Montgomery, Alabama (Friedman: 2005). For her act of defiance she was fined $14 and placed in jail. As a result, from December 5, 1955, African-Americans led by Martin Luther King Jr. formed the Montgomery Improvement Association (MIA) and boycotted the bus system for over a year in Montgomery even if it meant walking to work for some of its members (Anderson 2004: 52). Actions like these, however, helped spark the catalyst for change and the Civil Rights movement began to gain traction.

The NAACP had already been important in the Brown v Board of Education 1954 landmark decision by the Supreme Court (Anderson 2004: 51), whereby a black student, Linda Brown, was bussed out of the white neighbourhood in order to segregate her by making her attend a black school in Topeka, Kansas. The Court found the action to violate the Fourteenth Amendment, stating the differences in facilities were "inherently unequal" and that it lead to depriving children of the minority group of the education they deserved (Anderson 2004: 51). This action by the Warren Court was incredibly significant given its early role in fighting racially discriminatory practices and providing an equal level of access. Brown's situation was a result of the Jim Crow laws that were enforced in the Southern states of America maintaining a separate but equal status for African-Americans. Obviously this was seen as a palatable manner in which to segregate groups without having to acknowledge the reality that it created an underclass of society. Despite the ruling in 1954, many African-American students still attended what were essentially black schools well into the 1980s. This was usually due to the convenience of travel to a neighbourhood school, until many district authorities created schemes to help students pick a desired school, usually through a lottery scheme (Dubner 2006: 143). Even today, however, there still exists a large degree of naturally occurring segregation based on one's location as cultural groups tend to congregate (Dubner 2006: 151).

Action such as Rosa Parks and the NAACP response, coupled with landmark rulings such as the Brown decision, meant that by 1965 the Civil Rights movement was in full motion and was now able to demand equal opportunity in electoral democracy and opportunity for African-Americans, pressing for a policy of Affirmative Action aimed at aiding them to achieve these goals one day (Chateauvert 2000: 113-117). Affirmative Action's origins as a term are first cited in Executive Order 10925 (1961), issued by President John F. Kennedy (EEOC: 1961). The purpose of this order was to take affirmative action to ensure fair treatment in the application and employment period of a worker "without regard to their race, creed, colour or national origin" (Anderson 2004: 92), therefore attempting to ensure removal of discriminatory factors. This led to the establishment of the President's Equal

Employment Opportunity Commission (EEOC) in the Civil Rights Act of 1964 (Anderson 2004: 92-93). The movement argued this was a necessary step in order to combat racial discrimination. The reasoning being that the years of oppression had left the African-American community severely disadvantaged and that equal opportunity in employment and education access would not be fair and equitable given that African-Americans had been on the back foot for hundreds of years. As a result, in order for an African American to be equal within society it would likely take greater effort and work than their white counterparts who also had the advantage of dominant social networks. These kinds of social advantages and benefits that come with being a member of the dominant race provide the basis for the concept of white privilege. As part of his Great Society programme, President Johnson continued President Kennedy's work and put in place a legislative programme and presidential task force, with one of its aims being to address the Civil Rights issue. President Johnson issued Executive Order 11246 in September 1965 that stated large government contractors could not discriminate against race, as well as other grounds such as sex and religion, and that these contractors needed to take Affirmative Action to promote equality of treatment.

As a result of these actions, conditions began to improve for African-American and other minority groups. However, the 1978 Bakke case led to significant changes in how Affirmative Action policy could be applied to provide access for minority groups. In this case the University of California was found to have discriminated against Caucasians by having quota systems favouring minority students above Caucasians. The aim had been to quickly create a professional black middle class. However, the manner in which the University ran its admission policy violated the Fourteenth Amendment that provides equal protection and treatment (Anderson 2004: 150 - 151). As a result, the University was found to have essentially performed reverse-discrimination. The Court's decision meant that if a person was qualified, they should be allowed access regardless of race. However, the Court stated that they realised the rationale for these quotas was to atone for past discrimination but they could not allow for a new racial bias in the system (Anderson 2004: 152). However, the Court stated that systems such as Harvard's admission policy, which viewed race as a plus factor for admission and therefore added to the existing characteristics of an applicant, were permissible (Anderson 2004: 150-152). This decision was later supported by Grutter v Bollinger (2003) stating that student diversity at the University of Michigan Law School was a compelling interest to maintain their admissions criteria, though it deemed the system in place at the University of Michigan was too formulaic in the case of Gratz v Bollinger (2003) and would need adjustment as it resembled a quota system.

02 Crime and Merit

Those who claim reverse discrimination occurs often cite merit as an issue as to who should be employed. The concept of merit, one of the founding principles of the United States, is based on John Locke's work *The Second Treatise on Government.* It is the idea that one's effort and labour makes them deserving of reward. Michael Young book *Rise of the Meritocracy* attempts to formalise this concept further by stating merit is the sum of intelligence plus effort (I + E = M) for his fictitious account (Dench 2006: 8-11). As is concluded by Arrow et al. in their book *Meritocracy and Economic Inequality* (2000), merit cannot be measured accurately without the use of scaleable values and consequently they rely on economic output figures in their studies. This leaves much criticism as to how to measure accurately intelligence or effort and whether there is a need for Affirmative Action to be taken when the playing field may possibly be already equal.

Egalitarians often talk of Meritocracy in relation to elitist systems such as education (Arrow et al. 2000: 7) that place power in the hands of a minority with wealth or stature. Egalitarianism perceives equality as an important political value (Heywood 2002: 422). This view is often in contention with Libertarianism thought on Affirmative Action that prefers a limited scope of public authority so that individual liberty can be maximised (Heywood 2002: 425). Philosopher Stephen Hicks has commented on these competing ideologies of egalitarianism and libertarianism in relation to having racial or other group preferences for employment (collectivist principles) opposing ideas of individualism (Blumner 2002). Thus criticism of the policy is due to the perception it is not meritocratic and based on individual's ability, but based on collectivism (Chateauvert 2000: 112-113).

As a result, if Affirmative Action policy is implemented by legislation, it implies an asymmetry of power between groups of society. This puts it in a controversial position that may conflict the US constitution, particularly Article I that states "All men are created equal". If Affirmative Action is judicially mandated, then the preferential treatment one group receives cannot be equal. This has led to many court cases and legal action being taken such as California's Proposition 209 (1996) which meant that race, sex and ethnicity could not be considered by public institutions. This may be a reason why many institutions set goals for diversity rather than hold quotas.

The egalitarian view on Affirmative Action does not believe that all men are born equal. Due to the history of slavery and oppression in United States, African-Americans in particular are seen to be at a disadvantage with lower social capital than their privileged counter parts and, therefore, needing a policy program such as Affirmative Action to compensate for these hindrances.

The concept of social capital, its wealth creation and cultural networks aspects particularly are advocated by scholars such as Ronald Takaki as one of the reasons Affirmative Action is still required today (Halford 1999). Takaki argues that preferential treatment for minority ethnic groups is necessary as they remain at a socio-economic disadvantage even though it has been four decades since Affirmative Action was created. Takaki states that the majority of ethnic minorities live and study in inner-city areas which do not have all the benefit of *Advanced Placement* (AP) courses that can be found in many sub-urban schools which have a predominately white population. The ability to move to one of these suburban areas would require a person to have a high degree of wealth as they are economically affluent areas. AP courses allow students to achieve higher than 4.0 grade point averages (GPA). A 4.0 GPA is considered the maximum grade a student can achieve under normal comprehensive education conditions. However, with AP courses it becomes possible to achieve higher than 4.0 GPA scores such as a 4.2 GPA, the equivalent of getting 105% as a score, a better than perfect average score. GPA scores are given significant weighting by many universities in their consideration of applicants. This means if an ethnic student at an inner-city school achieves all A grades through his four years at high school, he may still be considered "uncompetitive" compared to a student from a suburban school who has not always received top grades but has instead been able to compensate or even surpass the 4.0 GPA by taking these additional classes (Massie: 2007). One of the primary reasons for this is the low social mobility of wealth. Keister (2000) states the existence of a distinct difference between wealth and income mobility and that high income does not necessarily correlate with high wealth. This suggests if a study focuses on income, it will not correctly account for the advantages wealth provides to a group, supporting Takaki's claims and other commentators such as Tim Wise who talk of White Privilege (Connerly 2006). As a result, where an individual lives can play a huge factor in increasing their chances of entry to a highly selective institute. Yet to increase these chances, they need to be living in an affluent area and would already come from a decent background.

Takaki also argued in his 2007 ISI debate that SAT scores are a flawed method of evaluating student merit, as there is vast correlative evidence showing that SAT scores are positively linked to family income and an affluent background, and their access to appropriate learning resources. This claim is backed by numerous studies such as Klein et al. (1997) and Ludwig and Bassi (1999). It is argued that left untreated the situation will exacerbate, with the socio-economic gap between ethnic minorities and non-ethnics increasing as social mobility will prevent a large enough segment of the minority population from breaking into better education and employment.

One issue Takaki does not address is the point that white students studying at inner-city schools also do not benefit from AP courses, yet will be forced to compete with students who have taken these courses in the university admissions process. In fact, within such schools there has been shown to be no difference between test score gaps for blacks and whites. It is only on a macro scale when varying quality of schools are compared that a difference can be seen between GPA scores. Therefore, if attending a low quality school, every student inside will suffer the same disadvantages. These schools are typically found in socially deprived areas, regardless of race (Dubner 2006: 151). However, the typical black youth comes from these socially deprived areas, as housing is cheaper in these areas, and consequently becomes a member of the low end of the socio-economic spectrum as deprivation is a typical characteristic of race in America.

Another major problem with this concept is that it holds many contemporary Americans as being responsible for actions they did not commit, many of those whose ancestors also may have been innocent, and as a result can be seen as being unfairly punished in the present by such a preferential policy as Affirmative Action based on the idea that the majority of white Americans took advantage of African-Americans in the past (Anderson 2004: 229). Historical liability of this kind allows for allegations of victimisation by reverse-discrimination proponents, claiming social determinism by one's background and the rejection of individual volition (Blumner 2002).

However, the declining admission rate of black minority students to the University of Calafornia at Berkeley since the passing and implementation of Proposition 209 suggests that the case for Affirmative Action still exists (Epstein 2006). Forty per cent of California is either African-American or Hispanic, yet only ten per cent of the University population is comprised of these groups (Massie: 2007). The percentage of the student population from these minority backgrounds has declined since the passing of Proposition 209. Darnell Hunt, head of University College Los Angels (UCLA) Bunche Center for African-American Studies echoes many of Takaki's claims that the reason for this is that many minority students are not considered as competing with the SAT scores or having higher than 4.0 GPA scores that non-ethnic minority applicant students have (Epstein 2006). Hunt further clarifies that UCLA has an even lower intake of minority students compared to Berkeley, despite being based in a county with the second largest concentration of African-Americans, due to their screening approach which relies heavily on looking at a student in terms of raw figures from SAT scores and GPAs. The more screening that occurs in this manner, the less likely it is that talented minority students are offered a place as their situation is not taken in context as the a compared to students who have taken AP courses or have high SAT scores. As a result, many of their rejects go onto institutions such as Princeton and Harvard which take a wider scope in their selection process.

Hunt states that this method is "systemically biased" against black students (Epstein: 2006).

Chung and Espenshade (2005) point out that the inherent belief that this kind of racial discrimination underpins low admissions of minority groups is flawed to some extent given that many universities given added weight to other student characteristics and other alternative means of entry such as sports scholarships. By stating that Affirmative Action receives a disproportionate amount of coverage, other aspects of university admission are overlooked. One of these traits is *Legacy* applications where the applicant's parent is a former alumnus and thus receives additional weighting and chance of entry, and that sports students are primarily white. Their findings show that there is an impact made against minority students place but this is relatively small.

Schotter and Weigelt (1992) have also commented that for an efficient and socially cohesive workforce and environment, there must be a perception amongst individuals that there is equality and access of opportunity to all. This reduces feelings of resentment and hate between societal demographics and consequently increases motivation and work effort rates. The reasoning behind this being if an individual feels that they will fairly be rewarded for effort and merit, then it is worth pursuing this route. When there is a belief of asymmetric treatment amongst the population, motivation levels can drop amongst the group that perceives discrimination. Subsequently, when a worker's motivation drops, there is a perception of lower energy and that they are not as productive by those in senior positions, which only perpetuates the problem. When applied to the area of further education in America, if students are conscious of the admissions system favouring students with AP courses, they may feel disenfranchised by the system and perceive further education as an inaccessible option.

When there is this perception of asymmetric preference or discrimination in the system of employment or access to education, criminologists suggest that it may lead to social disorganisation occurring through the weakening of mechanisms of social control. What this means from a sociological standpoint is that a person who feels that the system is against them has a greater propensity to turn toward criminal activity than one who believes they have level playing field and thus a greater number of options. An inability to enter work or education may also be associated with economic inequalities such as the income gap between low and high earners. This can lead to strain theory in which the relative success of others causes frustration on the part of unsuccessful individuals and may lead them toward crime as a means of compensating. Therefore, from a societal point, Affirmative Action could be used to help alleviate the occurrence of certain forms of crime from a perceptual point. Kelly (2000) particularly supports these views, and brings into focus the problems of an economic theory of crime, whereby areas of high inequality cause poor individuals with low returns from legitimate market activity next to high income individuals who have goods worth taking. Forst (1993) goes onto support such ideas by stating that statistically, African-Americans and other ethnic groups who tend to commit crimes are typically from low-income backgrounds when they undertake legitimate work.

Most crime is committed by young men and certain crimes such as property crime by teenagers in particular (Donohue 2001: 394). Education has been linked with reducing crime. One simple reason is that when a student is in education, they tend to spend more time at school or college, as opposed to having to fill their "free" time. The longer they are preoccupied with education, the greater their aspirations and goals tend to become due to a belief in their own merit. They also develop skills and qualifications that tend to lead to good jobs, and as a result are less likely to offend in future. However, a person's background can have an effect on their success in education, such as family circumstances, unemployment and social deprivation. However, this theory implies that psychological factors do not play a part in the criminal's intents and places some modelling assumptions into the behaviour of this type of economic evaluation (Bowmaker 2005: xxix-xxxi).

In the longer term, Becker's human capital theory implies that the number of years spent in education is negatively correlated with crimes that require little skill. This means the more skilled and competitive the workforce, the less likely it is they will turn toward crime. Depending on the level of education and ability, there is a point at which there is a return to white collar crime amongst the more educated. However, the proportion of people perpetrating this is far lower.

These results imply that the opportunity cost of committing a crime increases as people gets older, as their accumulated skills means they have more to lose should they be caught in criminal activity. This may be particularly true for individuals with a low mobility of labour skills who thus cannot easily switch into new roles (Bowmaker 2005: 101-103). As a result, the actual fear of being caught and the greater impact this may have on a person's life, the less likely they will be willing to risk their time outside of legitimate activity. Farmer and Terrel (1999) support the work of Schotter and Weigelt, and take the model further slightly, coming to the conclusion that both education initiatives and Affirmative Action (which encompasses equal access to education) lead to a reduction in criminal activity, particularly by disadvantaged groups, despite crime reduction not being a direct intended policy goal. This results from a better educated society being a more productive and thus affluent society. When society experiences a wealth effect, the crime rate fell, and that other social benefits such as greater equality and social cohesion are also experienced.

03 The Problem with being DeShawn

Affirmative Action now includes a wider spectrum of groups, and the focus is quickly moving towards the growing Hispanic population in America. However, since the 1960s, African-American culture has vastly expanded and this has certainly filtered down to other ethnic groups. Fryer and Levitt (2003: 1-6) point out that cultural divergence between white groups in society and non-whites has substantially increased over the decades. In Dubner and Levitt's book *Freakonomics,* the chapter based upon the work conducted by Levitt with Roland Fryer into black-white culture gaps shows that the cultural divide between what they term "blacks" and "whites" is so deep that of the top fifty television shows watched by blacks and whites, the only commonality is *Monday Night Football,* whilst television shows such as the sitcom *Seinfeld,* one of the most watched and highly commercial sitcoms in America and worldwide, does not even make the list for black viewers (Dubner 2006: 166). Evidence such as this has lead Fryer in particular to observe cultural factors against economic performance, believing that nurture and environment may have a bigger role than many assume (Dubner 2006: 166). Nadal (2005: 182-185) concludes that environmental factors such as television may impact society into having different values and perceptions of racial demographic groups, pointing to examples of African-Americans being portrayed as criminals on television reinforcing a specific stereotype. He also points to similar visual images influencing different segments of society in holding fundamentally different ideas about other cultures, thus Fryer's beliefs are supported to some extent.

A large number of audit studies by academics such as Holzer (2000) and Fryer (2006) have found the implications of Affirmative Action confirm that it is an effective policy in promoting employment for ethnic groups whilst also proving that quality of the workforce or student population is unaffected, discrediting claims of unworthy applicants receiving a job that is unmerited. As a result, it was established that prior to the policy's creation, many worthy ethnic applicants were underemployed resources and that there was a larger potential workforce available. When there is a larger skilled workforce, it is also harder for a group to claim for higher than average wages over another group for their ability level as there is a reduction of elitism within society[1]. This prevents discriminated against groups receiving a lower than deserved wage, and prevents those discriminating take a higher than deserved wage for their skill level (Chrystal 1999: 224-245). As a result, Affirmative Action policy has been effective to some extent in combating the problem of market failures, whereby they do not operate as efficiently as they should without the aid of external correction. Underemployed workers can be a result of inappropriate signalling mechanisms, such as lack of qualifications to show they are deserving of a job. However, in these audit studies, those employed were qualified and thus this was not the issue. Considering those in Holzner's research were already educated members from minority groups that were employed, it is not is not useful in

---

[1] See Diagram 1 in Appendix for further detail of the economic explanation for this.

detecting discrimination within the system. This is due to a fault in timing, the point at which data is collected is beyond the point at which discrimination preventing access to work would have taken place. A minority group member that is employed would have already overcome any problems of discrimination. Therefore, that type of research is more useful in proving that a minority worker is just as able as their non-minority counter part, but not at detecting discrimination. Many of these had also bypassed the issue of access to education, which, as was shown above, can have issues for access and strongly favours those from wealthier backgrounds. Despite the evidence of increased integration in society from these studies of the workplace, ethnic groups are still in the lower end of the socio-economic spectrum and there are still less of them employed in higher income jobs as a proportionally to their make up of society, suggesting that other factors may still be causing a problem (Chandra 2003: 34-36).

This has lead to claims of intrinsic racism in the system preventing access to education and employment. Racism is a pattern of thinking causing a perception among members of dominant groups to characterize members of non-dominant groups as being different or inferior in order to justify and result in lesser treatment or exploitation of the non-dominant groups. This means these non-dominant groups are not treated equally (Appelt 2000: 6).

The area of Affirmative Action has a lot of quantitative data on effectiveness and impact of the policy. Particularly large contributors to this field are economists at the American Inequality

Lab at Harvard such as Roland Fryer, Steven Levitt, as well as other prominent economists, including Nobel Prize winner George Akerlof. These works provide a high degree of correlative information that when combined with an appropriate formation of inductive reasoning and applied into a wider context can link to form a set of reasonable explanations to this field. While these works are important, for the most part they simply assess effectiveness and do not provide much argument for the creation or retention of Affirmative Action on their own. It is when these statistics are combined with a fairly substantive body of political work dealing with historical, normative and subjective views on Affirmative Action that have grown out of Civil Rights and Race works that the economic analysis become relevant.

Numerous "audit studies" have been conducted attempting to find evidence of discrimination being prevalent within the employment sector. This is typically done by creating two applications of identical calibre suitable for a job description with one having a traditional and non-ethnic name for that region and the other having a name that explicitly implies ethnicity or an ethnic background. Immediately such a methodology implies various limitations. For example, Michael Jordan is not a name that would necessarily imply any ethnicity, yet it is the name of a famous and successful basketball player. Jordan, however, was a gifted sportsman, and probably did not go through the type of screening processes that such a method would entail. Colin Powell's career would suggest that name is not a limiting function and, unlike Jordan, he operated within a far more conventional and rigid system. However, would Powell have been as successful had his name implied a more "black" background?

Recent audit studies such as Bertrand and Mullainathan (2004) have investigated discrimination at the application stage for a job. Due to this being at the application stage, it is more likely to show the effects of discrimination in the system. This study has shown that a name that is considered non-ethnic is likely to receive twice as many call-backs from applications as the ethnic names. However, these findings cannot prove that racial discrimination is the explanation for why this occurs and conflict with previous studies such as Holzer (1999) that show little evidence of discrimination in the system. As stated, the key difference is likely the timing of the data collection. Holzner researches the issue post employment, while Bertrand and Mullainathan investigate what happens to qualified workers in the employment process. Bertrand and Mullainathan's study did show when two applications are made with no indicators of cultural background other than name and the rest of the application is identical, an application that suggests a non-ethnic background receives a greater number of call backs. This raises the issue of whether a name can be used as a signalling mechanism to employers and whether they can then use this to screen out applicants. An ethnic name is one that has a higher number of incidences amongst one racial demographic of the population over another group proportionally. This means there is a greater concentration of that type of name within one group of society and by means of social osmosis, becomes associated with this group or culture.

Although there may be many explanations as to why the non-ethnic names receive a greater number of call-backs than ethnic sounding names, given quality is not a factor in these applications as they are identical in qualification, it suggests and signals that a non-traditional name for a society may have an associated set of assumptions placed upon them. If any of these assumptions have a negative connotation, this may lead to an economic penalty during the screening of applications for persons from these groups.

The growth of ethnic names can be attributed to the Civil Rights movements and the growth of ethnic identities. As a consequence, this is a fairly recent phenomena according to data. A girl born into an African-American background in the 1970s was likely to have a name that was only twice as common among this group compared to other groups in society. Therefore at that point in time, in terms of naming culture, African-Americans and white Americans were still very similar and would have had names that would not easily distinguish between the two groups. By 1980, it was likely that she would have a name that is twenty times more frequent amongst the African-American group than non-African originating groups (Dubner 2006: 167). This now meant that in terms of names, African-Americans were much more likely to have very different and very distinctive names compared to white Americans, and so their culture had become radically more pronounced.

As time has gone on, data shows that this departure in traditional Western names has increased and that there is greater variety amongst all groups in society, though greatest in ethnic groups. However, given that there has been an increase in name variation for all groups, most likely due to societal fashion and culture changes (Pharr 1993: 407), it can be explored what type of unwanted attention this highlights. This means that we can establish whether ethnic names themselves are the problem or untraditional names for any group.

Fryer identifies a phenomenon amongst the African-American population which he calls "acting black". This is the act of intentionally trying to show one's cultural and historical roots. Today seeing an Afro haircut or a man wearing a dashiki is rare. Once, these would have been an outward expression of someone's African heritage. Today a more likely place to spot this is in the name of a person. Though it should be noted, a person chooses to sport an Afro haircut or wear a dashiki but usually retains the name they are given from birth, typically by the parent(s), which is not their own choice. Since the Civil Rights movement, there has been an upsurge in distinctively different names between racial groups in American Society. This has resulted in different racial groups having a concentration of certain names that are more common within their own group compared to other racial groups. Therefore, if a sample population of society were taken, it would be found that some names occur greater within an African-American group as a ratio compared to the white American group, and consequently can be associated with African-Americans by culture.

From this it can be claimed that DeShawn is a very typical black name for boy, while Jake is the typical name of white boy in America (Dubner 2006: 169-170). If all the DeShawns in America were gathered together, the simple majority would be black. Research shows that Hispanics also have distinctive names, though not to the degree that African-Americans show, while Asians show a much lower deviation from traditional white American names. It should be noted that these studies focused on the impact on first name, probably because variation in surnames takes place due to them being passed on to each successive generation. However, a surname being generational may be just as easily be recognisable in some cases, hence why many persons of Jewish heritage have changed their name and consequently a reason why some people change their surname to have a Jewish sounding name, as was the case with one Indian born Sikh Taxi driver in New York city who renamed himself Michael Goldberg, believing it was more beneficial than his old Indian sounding name (Dubner 2006: 171-172). In the case of African-Americans, their surname may reflect the name of the person their ancestor was in servitude to. Whether or not this could allow a person to be screened as easily from surname has not been investigated, only distinctive first names that may imply ethnicity.

This claim over distinctive first (ethnic-originating) name theory now means it is somewhat plausible that an application form can imply a candidate of ethnic background when there are no other indicators of race or background. The name can thus act as a signalling device. To further strengthen these claims that discrimination is occurring within the system, Bertrand and Mullainathan (2004) conducted a series of tests with minor alterations made to the original experiment that they had conducted within their research. In one of the studies applications were sent including lower quality applications as well as higher quality applications of equal amounts with black sounding names (Lakisha Washington and Jamal Jones), and white sounding names (Emily Walsh and Greg Baker). Even with these modifications it was shown that for every call-back the ethnic name received, the non-ethnic name received twice as many (Bertrand 2004: 2-4). With this many call-backs favouring one group of society; it is easy to see how political and economic disparities between the white majority and other racial groups continue to prevail in modern society. As stated earlier, this method is limited to using the name as the only factor in employment, when in reality many jobs have applications as an early screening process before interviews. There is very little data on the ratio of ethnic employment and discrimination occurring at these later stages. Nor can it actually be ascertained for certain that discrimination was the reason the ethnic name applications fail. It also should to be borne in mind that an employer may call back an ethnic applicant with a non-ethnic sounding name. What occurs at these later stages, particularly face-to-face is far less examined, probably due to difficulties in collecting data at this stage and assessing whether an interview was conducted fairly and to an equal standard between any two applicants. Data could be recorded on how many white and non-whites applicants take interviews and their respective uptakes post interview. However, during this research no such data has been found. Data tends to be either application stage and post employment only. Considering that the applications were of equal calibre, this implies that if one possesses an ethnic sounding name, it holds an economic penalty. The audit study is too limited to address implications that a name may have on ones outcomes. There is certainly some link but these studies alone cannot provide a confident answer alone.

It is easy to assume these outward displays of culture in a name is the cause of the socio-economic disparity in America. However, Californian birth records hold a wide scope of useful information to this research, which may help establish a different hypothesis. Distinct ethnic sounding names are a reflection of the economic disparity between whites and non-whites according to Fryer and Levitt (2003).

The two economists came to this conclusion after their 2003 study which used data from Californian birth records. These birth records hold a high degree of data beyond typical birth records. Typical data, such as the baby's name, birth weight, gender, race and the parents' marital status were included, as well as additional items such as their zip code (postcode), method of paying the hospital bill and the level of education of the parent. This data can be used to build a wider picture of the child's background (i.e. their guardians' socio-economic background and the likely environmental conditions the child will be nurtured within). Birth weight can correlate with poor prenatal care, either through irresponsible parenting such as smoking and drinking while pregnant or insufficient dietary intake during pregnancy that usually occurs as an issue with lower-income families, thus it is likely the child will grow up in a poor household (Dubner 2006: 155-156). The zip code can reveal their address, and thus it is possible to ascertain their neighbourhood composition and likely socio-economic status. Their method of payment is an economic indicator, as in America healthcare is private with various payment and insurance options available to each segment of society. Finally, the education level of the mother at the time of the child's birth was included (Dubner 2006: 166-167). Fryer and Levitt examined sixteen million records using a regression analysis to correlate and compare different data sets and take the analysis of the signalling effects of names deeper and beyond simply signalling ethnicity.

Before the research had simply looked at what was a black name and what happened when this was used in a predominantly non-black environment. Fryer now researched what occurred to African-Americans with white names. The research had some interesting findings. Names such as DeShawn and Jamal were identified as popular amongst African-Americans. However, they were even more popular when the African-American group was further segmented into socio-economic groups. Low-end African-Americans living in black areas were more likely to name their children distinctively.

This lead the research to consider a new possibility, that naming fashion was related to a person's socio-economic background. In order to confirm these results, the research once again returned to the Californian data records, but this time examined white American names, and divided them into income groups. The results showed similar results to the black names. There were low-end white names and high-end white names. Just as DeShawn can be considered a black name, the name Cody can be linked to low-educated parents and a working class background, while a name like Benjamin is far more reflective of someone from a middle-class background.

As a result, distinctive names seem to be a trait of lower-educated parents (Dubner 2006: 177). A distinctively named child is usually the child of a low-income single parent with little educational background. If the majority of individuals born into these circumstances are able to be identified in the application process, they can never break out of the adverse conditions that are not conducive to generating socio-economically successful individuals (Dubner 2006: 173). In attempts to show that this type of name based socio-economic discrimination existed, Fryer and Levitt returned once more to the Californian records, but this time decided to trace back individuals' names to their heritage. Previously, the research had assessed the parents' background. Now it would trace back ancestry as far back as possible to see if background and class remained a consistent low factor. The results showed that low-end names of one generation tended to reflect the most common names of the middle-classes a generation earlier (Dubner 2006: 179). They explained this as a filter-down effect resulting from the working classes attempts at emulation (Dubner 2006: 183). However, one thing did show up clearly, as each generation of working class took up the middle class names, the middle class had already moved onto new names for that generation. As a result, it became possible to definitely correlate names with a class culture.

Fryer also argues in another paper, *"The Economics of Acting White,"* that blacks growing up in these areas and backgrounds have disincentives to work, as they will be deemed as selling out to a "white lifestyle" and is a reason they are less likely to take up education as seriously or extra-curricular activity such as ballet, compounding the problems they already face. Their environments are just not conducive to resulting in successful members of society. However, Levitt does go on to say in *Freakonomics*, that those who do study usually do so because they see the benefits and are not influenced into altering this belief (Dubner 2006:

146). In the same way that low-end white names have a distinctive nature, it may be possible and certainly plausible that those with low-end white names also live in socially deprived areas. If this is the case, then the problem shifts away from distinctive names signalling racial and ethnic discrimination to being one that shows class discrimination.

If we return to the audit studies, however, the ethnic candidate with their distinctive name has apparently overcome these adversities and yet has received a rejection despite being equally qualified as the non-ethnic equal receiving a call-back, then this explanation of discriminating against one's socio-economic background becomes extremely relevant. The reality is these audit studies are too inconclusive to confirm whether failure to receive a call-back is a result of racial discrimination, or if the name implies a person from a low-income and poorly educated family background, or possibly another explanation. This study cannot even confirm if the person screening the application is convinced or influenced into viewing applications as being from those from different cultures or backgrounds. How much attention is paid to the name in the application process is unknown. Hochschild (2002) states that the majority of Affirmative Action studies have huge holes in the corpus that can never be observed or measured accurately. It still cannot be ascertained if the reason for their rejection is racial discrimination or as described above, possibly showing a form of socio-economic background discrimination, despite the added information. Though a possible and important alternate explanation has been provided warranting greater examination, especially given many white working-class Americans feel they are being overlooked by the current system.

04 Remove Affirmative Action?

If the issue of African-American underachievement in the labour market and in education is more a problem of socio-economic discrimination as opposed to race based discrimination, many Affirmative Action directives may been seen as horribly misdirected in their aims and attempts to tackle fundamentally incorrect issues and, therefore, require correction. Class analysis from an Orthodox Marxist viewpoint tends to play down the importance of race, claiming race is simply a ruling class's weapon to oppress an entire socially non-dominant group (Eckberg 1980:15). This type of oppression as a result is not so much based on prejudice, as opposed to motivated by gain to the group performing the oppression, in this case, initially for capitalistic gains and later the discrimination likely shifted to a maintenance phase for what was perceived the dominant group in America (i.e. white Americans) (Eckberg 1980: 15-17). In reality white Americans should not have been the dominant group, wealthy white Americans should have been. However, perhaps due to their smaller numbers population wise, it became necessary to have working-class white Americans maintain their position indirectly by focusing their attention towards continuing the oppression of African-Americans, when in reality these working class white Americans were not in a drastically better position economically, only politically. As a result, two distinct forms of discrimination result for the two groups. Wealthy white Americans historically oppressed for economic gains that consequently helped them make political gains, while the later generations of working class white Americans could only oppress African-Americans and other ethnic groups in attempts to give themselves some political clout. However, in the American case, the oppression of blacks in the past for the benefit of wealthy white Americans, and its continuation in the wider society has lead to past-in-present discrimination, whereby neutral acts and practices in the present derive negative effects from the intentional past discrimination (Eckberg 1980:12). From a constructivist point of view it can be said that the different racial demographics of the working classes continues to perpetuate their existence by contesting each other. This means the problem evolves to become systemic in nature, and has likely resulted in part from the white working class never challenging those who benefited from not just oppression of blacks for personal gain, but also from the additional exploitation of the white working class themselves. As a result, those who held wealth historically continue to hold the majority of wealth and this wealth gap is still increasing. From 1960 to 1990, the top one percent of wealth owners increased their wealth further (Keister 2000: 262) While it is true that blacks suffered far worse conditions than their white working class counter parts, this was for the most part a result of an exacerbation of conditions that resulted from the white working class supporting the systemic exploitation imposed upon blacks by the white middle class. Race is used as a powerful tool in deflecting attention away from what can be considered the actual source of systemic failure in the society, as stated by Marxist theory. Eckberg and Feagin concluded that wealth inheritance and accumulation such as this needed to be addressed in more dramatic terms than Affirmative Action was currently doing (Eckberg 1980: 17-18).

Anti-racist essayist Tim Wise notes that even his opponents such as Ward Connerly do not oppose Affirmative Action, they simply question its need for being race-based in nature, leading to the question does systemic race discrimination still exist? Wise argues that recent studies into *The Effects of Social Networks on Discrimination in Salary Negotiations* have shown that much of the racism that continues to exist in the job market (both blue collar and white collar), due not because of explicit or malicious racial discrimination and intent, but as a result of the social networks the people in these jobs are immersed in. Consequently, those that can provide access to work tend to employ people who they perceive as being similar to them, which usually means white Americans. The problem being that due to the historical segregation between race communities, white Americans who have historically controlled jobs, have been surrounded by other white Americans and as a result continue to surround themselves with white Americans in the work world and in the places they live, for the most part unintentionally (Wise 2005). However, the ability of blacks and other ethnic groups being able to buy homes in what would be considered white areas may be reflective of their lower economic abilities. This essentially results in an "old boys' network" that is vital for landing the best jobs and especially government contracts. These networks exclude minorities irrespective of their ability, and thus help perpetuate the cycle of this socio-economic problem. In his debate with

Ward Connerly, Wise states that these networks are responsible for almost eight percent of contracts in America, citing that time after time the same few major actors dominate despite having poor track records of producing cost effective results (Connerly 2006). One explanation Wise offers for why this occurs is social conditioning and stereotyping that leads to racially disparate treatment. This is not racism, but the propensity to these views leads to racially impacting results (Wise 2005). Wise continues however to point out that these assumptions are likely the cause of racial tensions and distrust by pointing out an African-American is five times more likely to be wrongly convicted of a crime than a white American, a point that studies such as Farmer and Terrel (1999: 35) have confirmed.

Some opponents of Wise such as David Horowitz have stated that the black middle class is doing better than the white middle class of America now in terms of growth, and reducing the income gap disparity. Wise, however, points to this simply being the result of clever wording and showing the appropriate statistics. In terms of growth, the black middle class is currently growing faster than the white middle class. However, this is a result of the black middle class having had a greater capacity to grow into this class compared to the white Americans that has been entrenched there for longer. It is actually because positive steps have been taken that the black middle class has now begun to fulfil some of its potential as they once had stunted growth and being a sub-set of the population have greater scope for growth. While they are now growing at a faster rate, statistically

Blacks still have lower net worth, own less assets and have lower home ownership, and better resemble the white working class. Wise bases these arguments off from information found in *Black Wealth, White Wealth* by Melvin Oliver and Thomas Shapiro (Wise 2005). However, it should be noted that these arguments that Affirmative Action is working to reduce disparities are based on the growth of income for middle-class blacks. The effect on wealth is still relatively low, especially when taken as an average. (Wise 2005) This is hardly surprising when considering that someone like Oprah Winfrey is the wealthiest African American though in reality her wealth pales in comparison to many in America, and highlights the fact there is still a huge wealth gap in America. The effect on the working class is still rather low comparatively, likely due to Affirmative Action being a policy that primarily affects people's income, assuming that they have the ability to access higher levels of income your merit. This may become even more important in the future, given that there is now a large and growing Hispanic working class beginning to voice itself in America. If arguments for Affirmative Action are too narrowly viewed on race and more specifically the African-American experience, then other minority groups like the Hispanics could be left behind.

However, removing Affirmative Action cannot be seen as the answer. It has already been seen that since the passing of Proposition 209, there has been a decrease in black university students entering the Berkeley system. Therefore, it can be argued that with the system apparently against them, removal of Affirmative Action would lead to a decline in the aspirations of minorities.

Hicklin (2007) researched the effects of Proposition 209 and the *Hopwood* case by modelling how the outcomes of these could alter admissions in public universities. The results showed that the number of minority students attending university did not decline as a whole, it simply caused the percentage of minority students to decline in states that had highly selective methods of choosing its students, and redistributed them in states that had less selective measures[2] (Hicklin 2007: 337). This study supports what commentators such as Hunt and Takaki believed about the formulaic admissions system currently employed at

---

[2] See Diagram 2 in Appendix for correlation between increasing selectivity and a decreasing percentage of minority student uptake.

Berkeley systemically discriminating against minority students. The redistribution of minority students into other states also alleviates the problems of the reduced number of black students entering the Berkeley system, reducing concerns that it had completely reduced aspirations. However, it still raises some normative issues.

The original rulings and decisions for these motions were an attempt to achieve equality in opportunity and access for all members of society based on their merit. Yet, by doing so and making the system equal at the entry point, it leads to inequitable outcomes in the admissions process in reality and is detrimental in the longer term. This likely occurs because minority students have a tendency to come from lower socio-economic backgrounds that means they are not as privileged at the point of entry. Yet many students at the point of entry, while coming from a privileged background, are not responsible for their environmental factors for the most part. This leads to a massive problem of where to implement the policy and how to go about it, so that neither party can feel discriminated against.

In the world of work, despite equal qualifications, African-Americans are still not finding entry to work as often as white Americans if we take the audit studies to be reflective of the wider system. The important implication of the audit studies was that they gave strong indications that disprove reverse discrimination based on race occurs. If it is assumed that name could be used as an indicator of one's ethnic background, given that there are few well qualified minority workers, then it would have been these applicants who would have received a high proportion of call-backs compared to the white applicants, especially as qualified minority workers would be viewed as a commodity (Connerly 2006). It is as a result of studies such as these that Affirmative Action seems to have a stronger case for its continued existence in some form. However, its basis on grounds of race are not as strong given the discrimination may be related to socio-economic factors. Future audit studies should attempt to clarify if this is the case.

05 Assessing Affirmative Action

Affirmative Action still has argument for its need and continued existence. Equally qualified applicants to jobs from minority backgrounds are not receiving the number of opportunities in access to work and employment that non-minority appear to be. Similarly, this appears to be the case for students applying to highly selective institutes. When Affirmative Action policy is removed, models and current statistics indicate that access to some universities becomes restricted and forces students to go to institutes that might otherwise not have. This usually occurs as a result of minority students living in areas that are not affluent, and consequently do not have the same opportunity in their schooling to partake in classes that add points to a students GPA and allows many of them to compensate for a lack of ability.

The majority of minorities are in the low end of the economic spectrum, and typically working class. As a result, they find it difficult to break out of this situation as they lack the resources to do so. Without the policy in place, an already disproportionate situation continues to degenerate. The system consequently favours those that already hold a degree of access granted to them by their socio-economic background (income, wealth and culture). Without the policy, the rate of disparity between working class backgrounds and middle class increases.

There is also a sociological issue attributed to Affirmative Action as identified by Schotter and

Weigelt. Without a perception of equality of access and opportunity in the system, social cohesion declines and in turn leads to the negative perceptions of different demographic groups. There is a decline in the motivation levels amongst those that feel they are discriminated against, as they perceive a situation in which their aspirations cannot be met, and in turn leads the discriminators to perceive these people as lethargic and undeserving of the rewards that they benefit from. Removing Affirmative Action policy leads to a perception that the system is against minorities, and thus has become an interdependent part of the structural framework in America.

When there is a perception of equality and fairness of the system, it leads to greater aspirations amongst minority groups. This leads to them pursing greater levels of education. However, as has been seen, even when merited, minority workers face greater resistance to their entry into university admissions or the workplace. It is here that Affirmative Action is necessary to ensure those with the potential to become highly productive members of society are able to. When this occurs, there is a greater degree of wealth and affluence experienced amongst minority groups, social cohesion and reduction in crime is able to occur naturally. Those who are influenced by disincentives to work to begin with would likely never have succeeded anyway due to their mindset not attributing value to work and education.

The need for race based Affirmative Action still exists as African-Americans and other racially minority groups are still socio-economically deprived, and the research indicates that these conditions will not allow them to overcome this adversity alone. The only issue that weakens this argument somewhat is that there is also a large degree of socially deprived whites, as was found from the results of correlating an individual's name with socio-economic factors. However, Bertrand and Mullainathan's research showed that in terms of application screening, a white's low-quality application still would receive greater call backs than a black's, though the names they used in their study may not appropriately correlate with the qualifications they supplied. Thus it cannot be ascertained for certain whether these applications were rejected on a lack of merit, racial discrimination or the new possibility of a socio-economic discrimination.

The biggest issue remaining with Affirmative Action as it currently exists is the point at which to implement the policy in order to achieve equality of access and equitable outcomes. If the policy is implemented at the point of entry, it typically discriminates and is unfair towards non-minorities today who are not responsible for the circumstances of their background that have been shown to be important factors concerning entry to university admission in particular (and subsequently higher income jobs later in life). However, when the policy's effectiveness is reduced at the point of access, it leads to inequitable outcomes later on with students being redistributed to less selective and usually lower quality universities. This can as a result affect their ability to be seen as employable later on.

As a result, the effectiveness of Affirmative Action seems to be low, although it is a better scenario with the policy than without. This is in part due to there being a growing battle over Affirmative Action battle between Federal and State intentions. Federal actions attempt to provide a legal framework by implementing the policy in order to correct the societal asymmetries and State rulings usually lead to the Supreme Court constantly addressing the application of the policy in regards to the policy's application in Constitutional terms, weakening its impact in many places. This, however, in many cases may be seen as justifiable as many of these rulings have shifted the focus away from race based initiatives to more economic based ones that allow the policy to help a wider range of deprived individuals.

Affirmative Action has been shown to affect income more effectively than wealth. While this is a positive benefit, the biggest issue still appears to be that wealth is the major issue to be addressed, as the wealthy continue to get wealthier and increases in income to minority groups does not seem to be compensating for this. Wealth accumulation appears to cause greater impact than issues of racial discrimination, as no current policy can adequately deal with the impact wealth is having in terms of social capital and social networks. This research has implied a person's residence in an affluent area and coming from a better socio-economic background can have definite benefits, access to education, and possibly work, although this cannot be proved incontrovertibly at this time. Due to the limits of the scope of this investigation, housing and the impact of wealth were not directly investigated, though their issues and implications were discovered in order to provide answers to the research. Future studies should take these factors into account as they appear to be significant.

However, the issue of race should not be ignored. If discrimination is still prevalent in American society, as is indicated by the audit studies, then Affirmative Action has done little to address the underlying problem of racial discrimination. Interestingly, in order to resolve this, it is believed the best method would be to reduce wealth disparities between communities. The reason being this would allow greater mobility of cultures, particularly into what are already affluent areas as these minority groups would now be able to afford to live there. This would likely cause the social cohesion that is desired. This would also result in less socially deprived areas for all racial members of society, which may lead to a more productive society, reduced crime and an equality of perception between racial groups.

Appendix

Diagram 1

Illustrating the consequences of economic discrimination and its effect on the labour market.[3]

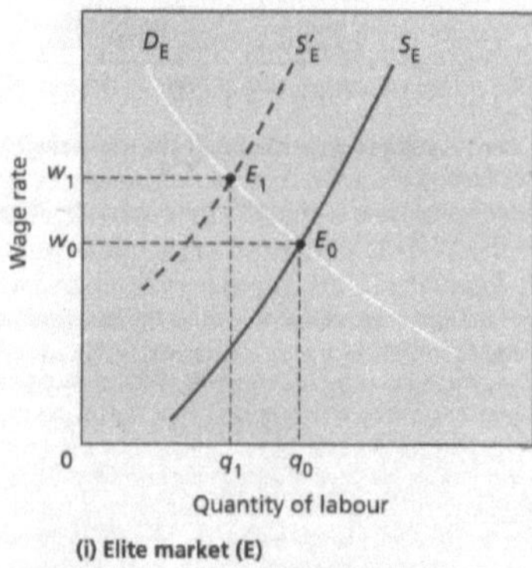

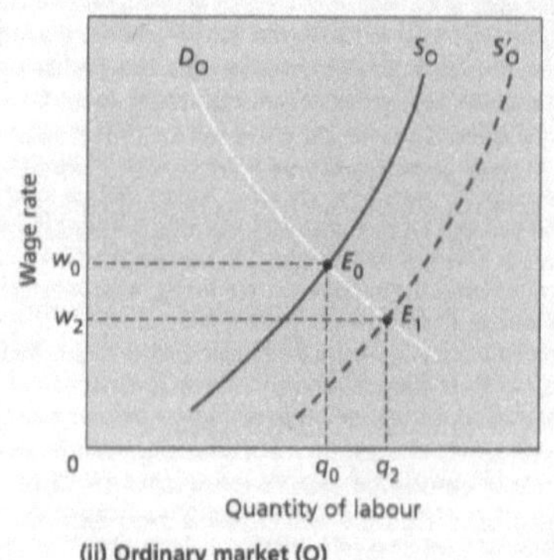

Figure 15.3 Economic discrimination

If market E discriminates against one group and market O does not, the supply curve will shift to the left in E and to the right in O. Market E requires above-average skills, while market O requires only ordinary skills. When there is no discrimination, demands and supplies are D_E and S_E in market E, and D_O and S_O in market O. Initially the wage rate is w_0 and employment is q_0 in each market. (The actual wage in market E will be slightly higher than the wage in market O.) When all Ys are barred from E occupations, the supply curve shifts to S'_E and the wage earned by the remaining workers, all of whom are Xs, rises to w_1. Ys put out of work in the E occupations now seek work in the O occupations. The resulting shift in the supply curve to S'_O brings down the wage to w_2 in the O occupations. Because all Ys are in O occupations, they have a lower wage than many Xs. The average X wage is higher than the average Y wage.

Diagram 2

---

[3] Diagram taken from Chrystal KA and Lipsey RG (1999) – *Principles in Economics Ninth Edition*, Oxford University Press (p. 244)

Showing the correlation between increasing selectivity in the admissions process and the percentage of minority students attending that institute in a hypothetical model for changes that occur in university admissions[4]

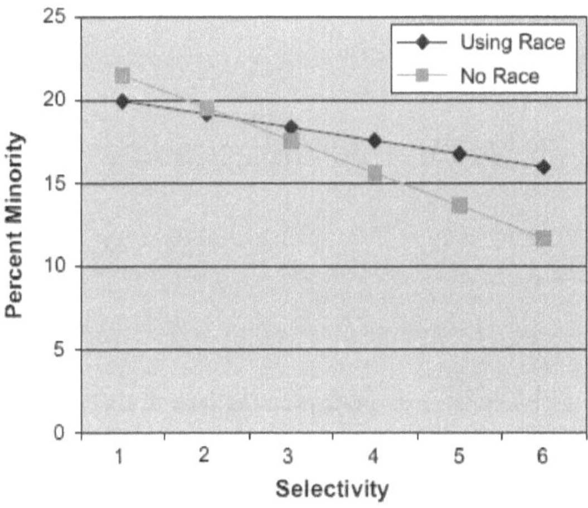

---

[4] Diagram taken from Hicklin A (2007) – "The Effect of Race Based Admissions in Public Universities: Debunking the Myths about *Hopwood* and Proposition 209", *Public Administration Review*, March-April, (p. 337)

Bibliography

Akerlof GA and Kranton RE (2000) – "Economics and Identity", *The Quarterly Journal of Economics*, Vol. CXV, Issue. 3, August, (pp. 715-753)

Arrow K et al. (2000) – *Meritocracy and Economic Inequality*, Princeton University Press

Anderson TH (2004) – *The Pursuit of Fairness – A History of Affirmative Action*, Oxford

Appelt E and Jarosch M (2000) – *Combating Racial Discrimination,* Berg

Barro RJ (2003) – *What's in a Name for Black Jobseekers,*

http://www.businessweek.com/magazine/content /03_44/b3856038_mz007.htm [13/01/2008]

Bertrand M and Mullainathan S (2004) – *Are Emily and Greg More Employable than Lakisha and Jamal? A Field Experiment on Labor Market Discrimination*, http://econweb.fas.harvard.edu/faculty/mullainath an/papers/emilygreg.pdf [15/10/2007]

Blumner RE (2002) - *The Competing Philosophies over Affirmative Action*, http://sptimes.com/2002/11/03/news_pf/Columns /The_competing_philoso.shtml [18/02/2008]

Brunner B (2006) - *President Johnson's Speech at Harvard University defining the concept of Affirmative Action*, http://www.infoplease.com/spot/affirmativetimelin e1.html 1965 [18/02/2008]

Bowmaker S (2005) – *Economics Uncut: A complete Guide to Life, Death and Misadventure,* Edward Elgar Publishing

Chandra A (2003) – *Is the Convergence in Racial Wage Gap Illusionary?* http://nber15.nber.org/papers/w9476.pdf [05/12/2007]

Chateauvert M (2000) – "Using Historical and Sociological Evidence to Defend Anti-Discrimination Policies", in *Combating Racial Discrimination* Edited by Appelt E and Jarosch M, Berg

Chung CY and Espenshade TJ (2005) – "The Opportunity Cost of Admission Preference at Elite Universities," *Social Science Quarterly*, Vol. 86, No. 2, June, (pp. 293-305)

Connerly C and Wise T (2006) – *Is Affirmative Action Good for America (Cicero's Podium: A Great Issues Debate Series)*, http://www.isi.org/lectures/lectures.aspx?SBy=le cture&Sfor=fd98aad7-97f1-461b-a598-4a85aebcb5fe 05/12/2006 [17/02/2008]

Chrystal KA and Lipsey RG (1999)– *Principles in Economics Ninth Edition*, Oxford University Press

Dench G (2006) – *The Rise and Rise of Meritocracy (Political Quarterly Special Issues)*, Blackwell Publishing

Donohue JJ and Levitt SD (2001) – "The Impact of Legalized abortion on Crime," *Quarterly Journal of Economics,* Vol 116, No. 2, (p.379 – 420)

Dubner SJ and Levitt SD (2006) - *Freakonomics*, Penguin Books

Eckberg DL and Feagin JR (1980) – "Discrimination: Motivation, Action, Effects, And Context," *Annual Review Social Sciences*, Vol. 6, (pp. 1-20)

Equal Employment Opportunity Commission (EEOC) (1961) - http://www.eeoc.gov/abouteeoc/35th/thelaw/eo-10925.html 06/03/1961 [11/03/2008]

Epstein D (2006) – *Struggling to Keep Black Students,*

http://www.insidehighered.com/news/2006/06/06 /black 06 June 2006 [18/02/2008]

Farmer A and Terrel D (1999) – *Crime versus Justice: Is there a tradeoff?* http://papers.ssrn.com/sol3/papers.cfm?abstract _id=189391 [18/03/2008]

Friedman MJ (2005) – *"Civil Rights Catalyst Rosa Parks Dead at 92"* http://usinfo.state.gov/xarchives/display.html?p= washfile- english&y=2005&m=October&x=200510251732 18jmnamdeirf0.7753918&t=dhr/hr-latest.html 25 October 2005 [05/12/2007]

Fryer RG and Loury GC (2007) – *An Economic Analysis of Color-Blind Affirmative Action,* http://www.economics.harvard.edu/faculty/fryer/papers/cbaarevision.pdf [16/10/2007]

Fryer RG and Levitt SD (2007) – *Testing for Racial Differences in the Mental Ability of Young Children,* http://www.economics.harvard.edu/faculty/fryer/papers/fryer_levittbabiesrevision.pdf [03/11/2007]

Fryer RG and Levitt SD (2003) – *The Causes and Consequences of Distinctly Black Names,* NBER Working Paper Series, 2003

Halford JM (1999) – *A Different Mirror: A Conversation with Roland Takaki,* http://www.ascd.org/ed_topics/el199904_halford.html April 1999 [18/02/2008]

Heywood, A (2002) – *Politics Second Edition*,
Palgrave Macmillan

Hicklin A (2007) – "The Effect of Race Based
Admissions in Public Universities: Debunking the
Myths about *Hopwood* and Proposition 209",
Public Administration Review, March-April, (pp.
331 – 340)

Hochschild J (2002) – "Affirmative Action as
Culture War", *A Companian to Racial and Ethnic
Studies* Edited by Goldberg DT and Solomos J,
Blackwell, (pp. 282-303)

Holzer H and Neumark D (2005) – *Affirmative
Action: What Do We Know?*
www.urban.org/UploadedPDF/1000862_affirmati
ve_action.pdf November 2005 [07/11/2007]

Holzer H and Neumark D (1999) – "Are
Affirmative Action Hires Less Qualified?
Evidence from Employer- Employee Data on
New Hires", *Journal of Labor Economics*, Vol. 17,
No. 3. Jul, (pp. 534-569)

Holzer H and Neumark D (2000) – "What Does
Affirmative Action Do?", *Industrial and Labor
Relations Review*, Vol. 53, No. 2. Jan 2000, (pp.
240-271)

Jones D (2005) – *"Evolving Issues: Racism,
Affirmative Action, and Diversity,"* in Unfinished
Business Edited by Wheeler MB, Scarecrow
Press, (pp. 43-55)

Massie M and Takaki R (2007) – *Is Affirmative
Action Good for America (Cicero's Podium: A*

Great Issues Debate Series),

http://www.isi.org/lectures/lectures.aspx?SBy=se

arch&SSub=title&SFor=affirmative%20action

29/03/2007 [16/02/2008]

Nadel A (2005) – *Television in Black-and-White*

America, University Press of Kansas

Pharr PC (1993) – "Onomastic Divergence: A

Study of Given-Name Trends among African

Americans", *American Speech,* Vol. 68, No. 4,

Winter, (pp. 400-409)

SASE (2007) – *The Society for the Advancement*

of Socio-Economics, http://www.sase.org/

[06/11/2007]

Schotter A and Weigelt K (1992) – *"Asymmetric*

Tournaments, Equal Opportunity Laws, and

Affirmative Action: Some Experimental Results,"
The Quarterly Journal of Economics, Vol. 107,
No. 2. May, (pp. 511-539)

SEP (2005) – *"Affirmative Action"*, Stanford
Encyclopedia of Philosophy,
http://plato.stanford.edu/entries/affirmative-action/ [04/11/2007]

Sowell T (2004) – "Affirmative Action in the
United States", *Affirmative Action Around the
World*, Yale University Press, (pp. 115-165)

Wheeler MB (2005) – *Unfinished Business*,
Scarecrow Press

Wise T (2005) - Discover the Nutwork David
Horowitz and the Politics of Ad Hominem
Distortion,

http://www.counterpunch.org/wise06152005.html

[18/03/2008]